# Blundermen *to* Wondermen

## Abraham Pulickal

WESTBOW
P R E S S®
A DIVISION OF THOMAS NELSON
& ZONDERVAN

WestBow Press books may be ordered through booksellers or by contacting:

WestBow Press
A Division of Thomas Nelson & Zondervan
1663 Liberty Drive
Bloomington, IN 47403
www.westbowpress.com
1 (866) 928-1240

ISBN: 978-1-5127-5897-9 (sc)
ISBN: 978-1-5127-5898-6 (hc)
ISBN: 978-1-5127-5896-2 (e)

Library of Congress Control Number: 2016916364

Print information available on the last page.

WestBow Press rev. date: 10/21/2016

# Contents

# *Preface*

The Lord has purposed my heart to write this book with the only intention of letting everyone know that there is nothing impossible with God, and when it is the matter or issue of our lives, the Lord can transform us from failures to victors and from the worst people we or the world knows to be the best people we or the world could ever have imagined.

The testimony of others always encourages us, and thus we will go through some wonderful testimonies from the Bible and also learn about some great men of our time and before—people the Lord did transform for His glory.

I remember the words of the wonderful hymn, written by Stuart Hamblen, which says:

> It is no secret what God can do,
>
> What He's done for others, He will do for you.
>
> With arms wide open, He will pardon you.
>
> It is no secret what God can do.

Also one wonderful verse from the Bible comes to my mind right now which says:

> If My people who are called by My name will humble themselves, and pray and seek My face, and turn from their wicked

ways, then I will hear from heaven, and
will forgive their sin and heal their land.

—2 Chronicles 7:14 NKJV

Today is your day. This chance is yours to be
transformed and renewed, to gain strength and
victory, and to become the blessing God had always
intended you to be.

*Chapter 1*

# Called to Be Blessed

God created man in His own image and blessed him with all the blessedness he needs in his life.

The Lord God has planned and purposed blessedness for all.

> For I know the thoughts that I think toward you, says the Lord, thoughts of peace and not of evil, to give you a future and a hope.
>
> —Jeremiah 29:11 NKJV

The devil is constantly working in the hearts and minds of the people, and he desires that they should fail in their lives and ultimately foil the wonderful plan of God in their lives.

There are many people today who have more than enough money, luxury, and fame, yet still their lives are empty. The void and the loneliness in their lives can be filled only by God.

There are many who are successful in their academics or in their businesses, yet their personal or family lives are disasters and failures.

The devil is entering the hearts and minds of the people, encouraging them to experiment with all the evil things in their lives, waste away their time, and stay away from God.

Men and women who were created as wondermen and wonderwomen by God are now being targeted by the devil. The devil has destroyed their lives and has instead made them blundermen and blunderwomen.

Yet our gracious, benevolent, loving, and all-powerful God has not given up on us, and in transforming all the failures into successes, He will also transform all the blundermen and blunderwomen again into wondermen and wonderwomen.

God has called us and made us to be blessed, and He will restore us back to our blessedness.

There are many things that worry us in our lives, yet this is what the Lord has to say to us always:

> Be anxious for nothing, but in everything by prayer and supplication, with thanksgiving, let your requests be made known to God; and the peace of God, which surpasses all understanding, will guard your hearts and minds through Christ Jesus.
>
> —Philippians 4:6–7 NKJV

Our anxiety will be turned into peace when we learn to pray and commit all our cares and worries to the Lord God. For this is a wonderful offer from the Lord God to us:

Cast your burden on the Lord, And He shall sustain you; He shall never permit the righteous to be moved.

—Psalm 55:22 NKJV

Casting all your care upon Him, for He cares for you.

—1 Peter 5:7 NKJV

The Lord has not left us as orphans; He is with us always as a loving heavenly Father who knows us and understands our needs.

By committing ourselves into His blessed hands, we are ensuring that we will receive the best, for He has made us, and no one knows us better than He.

Our God is all powerful and thus can bring us out of any circumstance or condition that we might even think is impossible to overcome, for there is nothing beyond His control.

If we desire the best to happen to us and to our families and loved ones, we need to come to the best, bring our families and loved ones to Him, and He will transform us in a glorious and miraculous way. And when He executes the change in us and in our lives, the devil cannot destroy Him or His plans in our lives, for the Lord will accomplish and fulfill His task for us.

> For the Lord of hosts has purposed, And who will annul it? His hand is stretched out, And who will turn it back?
>
> —Isaiah 14:27 NKJV

Today, humanity's alienation from God is our biggest problem, for if we are with God and live in His perfect will always, then we will never fail and will always have hope, for "Christ in you, the hope of glory" (Colossians 1:27 NKJV).

*Chapter 2*

# Moses

Born into a humble Hebrew family but reared up in a palace arrayed with all glory and strength, the Prince of Egypt once used his strength to quiet an Egyptian soldier, yet he had to pay with all his royalty and become a vagabond, finally to settle down in Midian as a shepherd for the rest of his life. This was the identity of Moses until the Lord called him with a mighty calling for the glory of His name.

Moses was powerful, well educated, and a great orator (Acts 7:22); he had all that was needed to become a great leader. And so in all his strength and glory, he tried to rescue a fellow Israelite by killing an Egyptian soldier (Exodus 2:12). Is he not similar to many of the leaders we find in today's world? Do they not try to rule by their strength and power? Do they not put to silence anything and everything that comes in their way to vainglory?

We might often think, from where do these wars arise in the world? Who or what is the source of all this dissipation and dissention? The Bible has an answer to this:

> Where do wars and fights come from among you? Do they not come from your desires for pleasure that war in your members? You lust and do not have. You murder and covet and cannot obtain. You fight and war, yet you do not have, because you do not ask.
>
> —James 4:1–2 NKJV

What a blessed fact to know that the alternative to war, hatred, and strife is prayer. We can have more and better in our lives through prayer than through war. Thus, in the time of your need, do not run around fighting or pleasing people and seeking favors; rather, you should pray, and the Lord God will open a way out and bring the required redemption.

Moses used his strength, yet the much-awaited appreciation for this heinous act actually turned into fear when he was required to run for his life.

God wanted a different leader in Moses, and thus He let Moses run away. Yet Moses's steps were directed by the Almighty, for the compassionate and loving eyes of the Father follow us wherever we go or are sent. The next forty years of Moses's life were a training session for humility; God wanted all of Moses's pride, arrogance, and dependence on his own strength to go away. And then, when he was ready as an empty vessel to receive from the Lord His strength and power, the Lord would fill him and use him for His glory.

There is a wonderful poem about how the Lord converts those whom He calls and desires to use for His glory.

*Abraham Pulickal*

## When God Wants to Drill a Man

When God wants to drill a man,

And thrill a man,

And skill a man

When God wants to mold a man

To play the noblest part;

When He yearns with all His heart

To create so great and bold a man

That all the world shall be amazed,

Watch His methods, watch His ways!

How He ruthlessly perfects

Whom He royally elects!

How He hammers him and hurts him,

And with mighty blows converts him

Into trial shapes of clay which

Only God understands;

While his tortured heart is crying

And he lifts beseeching hands!

How He bends but never breaks

When his good He undertakes;

How He uses whom He chooses,

And with every purpose fuses him;

By every act induces him

To try His splendor out-

God knows what He's about.

—Anonymous

God has His own and unique way of healing us, yet the fact is that in all He does to us, He is actually healing us and leading us to perfection.

When the Lord was sending away His beloved people into captivity, these were His words to those whom He was punishing:

> For I know the thoughts that I think
> towards you, says the Lord, thoughts of
> peace and not of evil, to give you a future
> and a hope.
>
> —Jeremiah 29:11 NKJV

Truly, God knows what He is doing, for even when He hurts us, He does it for our benefit.

Now, when asked whether he was ready to go down to Egypt and stand before the pharaoh to seek the deliverance of God's people, Moses found himself stammering; he could not speak fluently (Exodus 4:10). His strength had gone, for now he was eighty years old, and everything in him and around him disqualified him to be the leader Israel was looking for.

Yet God has His own way of selection and election, for He strengthens the weak and feeble hearted and is able to perform great and wondrous acts through them:

But God has chosen the foolish things of the world to put to shame the wise, and God has chosen the weak things of the world to put to shame the things which are mighty.

—1 Corinthians 1:27 NKJV

For now the time had come to move in His strength, which never fails. And the time had come to move in His command and in his Word—which shall never pass away.

The world might have concluded that Moses was the perfect example of a failed man—a man who made the blunder to try and rescue himself by his own strength only to fail and never rise again, living the rest of his days a poor stammering shepherd.

How much should we thank God for coming after us, seeking us, and searching for us? For He knows how to create beauty from these ashes, and if He did it for Moses, He can do it for you too.

If you and all those around you have concluded that you, like Moses, are "never to rise again," then I would encourage you to commit your life and circumstances into the hands of the Master and let Him give it a try. Let Him take you into His blessed hands and do what He can, and I am sure that there will arise the most beautiful and blessed part of your life.

Moses went back to Egypt with the strength of the Lord. He had no royalty, eloquence, or power to back him, yet what he had was the divine calling, the power of God, and the assurance of His presence.

When Peter and John saw the lame man sitting at the temple gate in Acts chapter 3, Peter said this to the lame man:

Silver or gold I do not have, but what I have I give to you. In the name of Jesus Christ of Nazareth, rise up and walk.

—Acts 3:6 NJKV

And the man was healed.

Do you think that silver or gold would have benefitted him more than his healing? Even today the best deed the rich and the successful can do is to lend out little silver and gold and nothing more, yet it takes the anointed of the Lord to give the best that is needed. Today, the world needs healing more than it needs silver and gold. The world needs Christ more than it needs riches.

Moses, who had been afraid forty years before, was now feared and looked upon with respect by Pharaoh and the other Egyptians, for God had brought about this change, God had honored him.

The Lord God had brought about this amazing transformation in the life of Moses, and He can do the same for us too. What the Lord needs is a willing heart and a humble spirit. He needs us to be obedient and submissive to Him always.

Moses was no more the blunderman he used to be; the Lord had changed him and made him the wonderman forever.

*Chapter 3*

# David

All who have carefully studied the Bible cannot be ignorant of this great man who was also called by God as 'a man after My own heart' (Acts 13:22).

Chosen and anointed at a very young age, a great songwriter, composer of the most beautiful and blessed Psalm 23 and many other blessed songs, and the mighty victor in many battles—that's who was King David.

Yet, the devil drove David into the dungeon of sin and tried to lock him there. However, the Lord had a wonderful plan and purpose for David's future, and when David came back to the Lord in perfect humbleness and submission, the Lord forgave his sin and blessed him.

The Bible gives this option to everyone saying:

> That if you confess with your mouth the Lord Jesus and believe in your heart that

God has raised Him from the dead, you will be saved.

—Romans 10:9 NKJV

David did commit the sin of adultery. He tried to cover it up in vain by getting Uriah, husband of the woman with whom he committed the sin, killed, yet the Lord Who knows the secrets of our hearts sent His prophet Nathan to David. Nathan told him that his God had seen him.

David did not waste even a moment and did not carry on with his cover-up; rather, he confessed and sought the Lord's pardon.

The Lord, who is compassionate and merciful, slow to anger, and abounding in loving kindness, forgave David and restored his joy.

David, for all of us, is a perfect example of a common man with common ways and means praising God's perfect way. David's experience is a perfect example of how God can change a man and exalt him to eternal glory for the entire world to see, and how God can give a permanent inheritance and an exalted name to someone who is not important for anyone, even for his parents.

We too might be facing the same rejections in life; we too might have felt ignored by our most loved ones. Yet, the good thing in all this is that the God of David is still alive and is our God also; He will do the same for us too.

Often in our lives we might have done works or deeds that were sinful and hurt God, yet later, did we correct these transgressions? Did we reconcile with our beloved Lord?

The most important, vital, and necessary thing is that we should come back to God.

God's pursuit for the whole world today is that we get back to where we belong; we are created in the image of God, and God wants us to come back so our lives may reflect His glory and goodness.

Often the guilt of sin pierces through our heart, makes us feel miserable, and drops us down in deep despair. Only God can bring us out from there. Here are the very words of Jesus:

> Come to Me, all you who labor and are heavy laden, and I will give you rest.
>
> Take My yoke upon you, and learn from Me, for I am gentle and lowly in heart, and you will find rest for your souls.
>
> —Matthew 11:28–29 NKJV

This verse tells us that God knows our condition and is calling us for restoration. Our God is not like the world, which may find us in our despair and miseries and leave us there to suffer. He is willing and able to bring us back to perfect peace and happiness.

Complete peace and happiness will come to our souls when we receive the yoke of God in our lives. Receiving the yoke of God is not receiving a burden; rather, it is submissively rendering us to the very purpose of our creation and the fulfillment that will bring the greatest satisfaction, peace, joy, and solace to our soul.

There were many experiences in the life of David that literally brought him near to death or to utter ruin, yet he arose from all of them and came out as a victor just for this very cause, about which he blessedly sang in his most favorite song:

> Yea, though I walk through the valley of
> the shadow of death, I will fear no evil;
> For You are with me;
> Your rod and Your staff, they comfort me.
> —Psalm 23:4 NKJV

The presence of God is all that matters in our lives.

We too might have committed blunders as David did, yet each of us, too, can become the wonderman he became through God, who made him the greatest king the world has ever seen.

*Chapter 4*

# Samson

This man was arrayed with strength, beauty, and blessedness from his birth, as he had a special calling from God in his life. His parents did well when they told him who he was and to whom he belong, yet walking in this sinful world, Samson could not resist the lust of temptation that flowed around him, and he often succumbed to his temptations.

The Lord delivered Samson from many such temptations by the anointing he had; yet when he touched upon the basic requirements of his calling, he lost the presence of God. Yet later, as we commonly read in the biblical language, "when he came to his senses" (as in the case of the prodigal's son), the Lord restored his strength for the last time.

Here are some of the things we can learn from the life of this great saint of God:

1. Know your calling and live up to it.

2. Your strength comes from God alone.

3. Never play with your anointing; you cannot travel in two boats at a time.

4. God is compassionate and longsuffering.

5. Know and ensure that your best is always in God and for God.

Let's address these points one at a time.

## 1. Know your calling and live up to it:

> Therefore, brethren, be even more diligent to make your call and election sure, for if you do these things you will never stumble.
>
> —2 Peter 1:10 NKJV

God called Samson with a very special calling as a judge for His people. Samson was called to lead the people of God and rescue them from the Philistines. Even though the Lord empowered him with His strength and His Spirit, Samson did not live up to his calling.

When God calls us for His purpose, He has great and blessed expectations from us. He wants to use us as vessels into which he can pour His abundant love and goodness. The Lord plans through us, yet when we make ourselves unavailable for His blessed tasks, the Lord's work is hampered, and His plan is disrupted. The Lord wants to continue His blessed task; however, the blessedness that would have come to us for being the chosen vessel of God would be lost to us. We would lose this blessed privilege.

The Lord wants to see us be faithful to His blessed calling. That which is holy unto the Lord cannot be unholy and wander the whole world bringing disgrace to the name of the Lord God. The Lord wants to build upon us His blessedness, yet when we ourselves are bent on self-destruction by corrupting our spiritual life, how can God bless us and make us a blessing for others?

We should know who we are, and we should recognize the blessed task for which we have been called, for God expects much from us. There is much ground to cover, there are many souls to be saved, and our blessed lives should shine for God and remove the darkness from the lives of many of our brothers and sisters.

We are the salt of the world and are required to maintain our saltiness. If we choose to give up our flavor and our anointing, we will drop down to be trampled underfoot by the world (Matthew 5:13).

The purpose of light is to shine. In doing so, it removes the darkness. Yet, when it chooses not to shine, like it or not, the darkness will overpower it and blow it out. All the time it is shining, it is overpowering; however, the very wrong choice of compromise will blow it out and make it useless.

Having received this great blessedness, how then can we preserve it? By enlightening ourselves constantly from the Great Light (in prayer) and by flavoring ourselves constantly by the Bread of Life (study of the Word of God). The little children sing the fact when, with innocent hearts, they sing in their Sunday school "Read your Bible. Pray every day. And you'll grow, grow, grow. Don't read your Bible. Forget to pray. And you'll shrink, shrink, shrink" (author unknown).

## 2. Your strength comes from God alone.

> Thus says the Lord, "Let not the wise man glory in his wisdom, let not the mighty man glory in his might, nor let the rich man glory in his riches, but let him who glories glory in this, that he understands and knows Me that I am the Lord exercising loving-kindness, judgment and

righteousness in the earth, for in these
things I delight," says the Lord.

— Jeremiah 9:23-24 NKJV

Samson had his strength from God; however, he never cared to use it for God. On the contrary, he misused it for his own purpose. God is the only source of all blessedness in our lives. We can never ever boast about our strength, for it is by the grace of the Lord that He has empowered us, and He desires us to use our strength for His glory.

Often when we are empowered with God's strength, we forget that He who has empowered us can also take back what He has freely given. If he were to do that, then our condition would be much more miserable.

There is no source of blessedness other than God. Our own abilities have limitations, yet that which God gives is perfect and complete.

Samson performed mighty deeds, yet he did them only when he was empowered by God's Spirit. However, when he acted against the will of God, the Lord took away His anointing and strength, and Samson was reduced to a common man. Samson had himself caused his own ruin.

The Lord blesses us. He empowers us so that we may work for His glory. With the power from the Lord, our every act should be to bring glory to His holy name and spread the love of Christ to others. When we make our every move for God's glory, the Lord strengthens us with even more gifts, talents, and opportunities for His glory. Yet in all this, let us bear in mind that He is the source, and If we forget, ignore, or displease Him, then we are cutting off our own source of blessedness.

### 3. Never play with your anointing; you cannot travel in two boats at one time.

Your anointing is the most precious and blessed thing that God has given you. You should feel privileged to receive this anointing from the Lord. Because it comes from Him, you should never play with your anointing; rather consider it precious and use it in the way the Lord wants you to use it. Samson was called to be a nazarite. He knew very well the rules he had to follow to fulfill the required vows, yet he chose to ignore them. He neglected them and handled his anointing his own way rather than the way the Lord required of him. Samson touched a dead body, went after heathen women, and thus lost his anointing.

Often we who are called to lead the world to Christ are pulled by the attractions of the world to our destruction; we succumb to the temptations of the devil and allow our minds and bodies to do sinful acts of foolishness.

The great man of God, King David, also knew the worth of this blessed anointing; thus, when he sinned against God, this is how he prayed repenting for his sins:

> Create in me a clean heart, O God, And renew a steadfast spirit within me. Do not cast me away from Your presence, And do not take Your Holy Spirit from me.
>
> —Psalm 51:10–11 NKJV

God has made us holy and called us to maintain our holiness so we will be like Him. The devil, being our enemy, visits us often with his latest sinful offers to deceive us and tempt us to sin, yet we are required to resist him and be holy unto God.

## 4. God is compassionate and longsuffering.

There is no one like our Lord, for He is merciful and compassionate, always ready and eager to forgive and restore.

It is rightly said that, even if we move away from God and drift a million miles away and then come to our senses and repent, when return, we will find God waiting just next to us.

God's eyes are always upon us, even when we are in sin, and thus it is said:

> But God demonstrates His own love toward us, in that while we were still sinners, Christ died for us.
>
> —Romans 5:8 NKJV

God seeks our welfare, and thus He wants us to return to Him, for He is compassionate and gracious, abounding in mercy, slow to anger, and abounding in love.

Samson did sin against God, yet at last when he repented, the Lord forgave him and blessed him. This does not mean that we can play the "sin and repent" game with God. For it is written:

> He who covers his sins will not prosper,
> But whoever confesses and forsakes them
> will have mercy.
>
> —Proverbs 28:13 NKJV

Even today, the Lord wants to forgive us for all our sins and iniquities, if we genuinely repent and seek Him with all of our heart and soul.

One of the things that God cannot do is that, He cannot turn a deaf ear to a repentant sinner.

## 5. Know and ensure that your best is always in God and for God.

It has been rightly said by George W Truett that "There is no failure in God's will, and no success outside of God's will". We are the best when we are perfectly walking in God's will. Most of the misery, sorrow, and problems in the world and also in the individual lives of its inhabitants happen only because we have chosen to live outside the will of the Lord and thus unknowingly have invited in all the filth and dirt, which has choked our society and families to death.

We need to know God's will for our individual lives, our families, our communities, and for society as a whole, and we need to take care to walk in His will.

The scripture rightfully says:

> But without faith it is impossible to please Him, for he who comes to God must believe

that He is, and that He is a rewarder of those who diligently seek Him.

—Hebrews 11:6 NKJV

We have to completely trust and believe in God and believe that He is the One who rewards all good things in our lives.

Having now realized that our best is in God, we need to endeavor to also give our best to God.

The reason we need to give our best to God is that He well deserves it. For all that He is and has done for us, our Lord deserves our best love and devotion.

The secret of receiving the best from God is to give our best to Him, failing which we will fall off the platform of holiness and faithfulness on which the Lord distributes His blessings and goodness.

It is not a give-and-take relationship; rather, it is honoring the worthy. When God honors us, the unworthy, to make us worthy, we need to honor God, who is, was, and will always be worthy.

We need to completely offer our lives to God. We need to boldly proclaim His holy name. We need to live as perfect witnesses before the whole world and display the love and goodness of the Lord.

Samson sought worldly deceptions only to receive deceit and failure, yet when he returned to the Lord God, he experienced the goodness of the Lord.

Samson killed many more people during his death than he did when he was alive.

The blunderman that the devil wanted him to be had returned to be the wonderman God always intended of him to be.

*Chapter 5*

# Jacob, Supplanter to a Prince

Jacob was a very clever and cunning man born to a very clever and cunning mother who always favored him and almost ruined his life.

Rebekah, the mother of Jacob, was very bold. She showed this at the time of her marriage when she gathered courage and strength to go with a stranger to meet her bridegroom. She also showed it later when she encouraged Jacob to steal the blessings of Esau, his twin brother.

Jacob also depended on his strength and kept running away from brother to father, from father to uncle, from uncle back to his land, and then to his brother, and at last to father Isaac after almost twenty years.

All through this span of twenty years, he cheated everyone right and left intending to save himself by fooling others. Only later did he realize that he had been making a fool of himself.

Often we do the same thing. We tell one lie after another, play one trick after another, cheat one time after another, and then we go around as if in an infinite loop not knowing how to free ourselves.

Jacob had to halt at one point. He let go of everything he had, and then when all was gone and he was alone, he wrestled in prayer with God at the Jabbok River (Genesis 32:22–32). The result of Jacob's prayer was not that God changed all who dealt or would deal with him; rather, as Jacob wrestled in prayer, God changed him. The Lord touched the socket of his leg so that Jacob could not run anymore, and then He changed his name from Jacob (a supplanter) to Israel (a prince with God).

When everything seems to be moving so fast in life and things get out of control, we need to pause what we are doing and spend time in prayer. We need to open our hearts to God and let Him deal with us. We need to acknowledge our frailty before God and seek His providence to lead a better life filled with peace and solace.

We cannot run away from everyone and everything and be safe. We can be safe only when we run to God from where we are and seek refuge in Him. The Bible says:

> The name of the Lord is a strong tower;
> The righteous run to it and are safe.
>
> —Proverbs 18:10 NKJV

Jacob had almost finished his marathon race and was about to meet the person he had first cheated, who was his own brother. Having heard the news that his brother was coming to meet him with almost four hundred people, Jacob felt a deep need to seek the help of the Lord. And the Lord did not reject him; rather, the Lord did an awesome miracle for him:

> When a man's ways please the Lord, He makes even his enemies to be at peace with him.
>
> —Proverbs 16:07 NKJV

When Esau came to Jacob, instead of crushing and killing him, he embraced him and loved him.

We can never predict the wonderful ways of the Lord; we can just be close to Him and experience His blessedness.

Jacob's life was spared, and he was saved then and forever. His fears were gone, and the cheater blunderman was transformed into a blessed wonderman who had received the Lord's forgiveness and goodness.

Jacob's experience at the Jabbok River was awesome. It changed his life, and I strongly believe that we all should have similar experiences that teach us that there is a need to let go of all that we possess. Only then can we be the real and authentic individuals we are before God. When we sincerely stand alone before God, we will feel the deepest need of His goodness, and we will see the frailty of all our self-strength and abilities.

Paul said,

Therefore I take pleasure in infirmities, in reproaches, in needs, in persecutions, in distresses, for Christ's sake. For when I am weak, then I am strong.

—2 Corinthians 12:10 NKJV

The conviction of our deepest need will become for us our greatest strength when we address this to God, for God Himself will fill in for our weakness and empower us. This empowerment will be the best thing that could ever happen to us.

Jacob could not run as he had been able to before his experience. He experienced a need to depend on God to move him forward, and that is much better.

Moving slowly in God's strength and His perfect will can provide much more for us than running speedily in our own strength and ways.

Jacob ended up walking in God' strength.

The supplanter had been changed to be a prince with God—the blunderman had changed to a wonderman for God.

*Chapter 6*

# Zacchaeus

Zacchaeus was chief of the tax collectors. To use a phrase that was famous in his time, he was "chief of all the thieves and cheats." Zacchaeus had gathered a great deal of money through ignoble activities in an attempt to find ultimate peace and solace; however, his soul was still thirsty and hungry for the living God.

Like Zacchaeus, many people in today's world try to fill in their lives with money instead of God, and thus they end up ever wanting and experiencing a void in their souls. Nothing can fill in for God in our lives; we were made in the image of God, and we were made for God.

Zacchaeus had heard about Jesus and had learnt about how different were the ways of Jesus when compared to his own ways. This made him curious to know more.

Jesus was not popular as a wealthy person; however, He was known as a mighty healer and miracle worker. For this reason, Zacchaeus wanted to see Jesus.

There was a large crowd of people, and Zacchaeus was very short, so he made his way up into a sycamore tree and safely hid himself among the leaves. Zacchaeus was an expert at hiding, and no one as yet had been able to catch him red handed; thus for him, hiding from Jesus was not a difficult task. He safely mounted himself on the sycamore branch and had a good and full view of Jesus. He had perfect plan: he would come down from the tree after having seen Jesus and then return to his normal affairs of life indulging in cheating and stealing and fraud. Zacchaeus had never imagined that the convoy of Jesus would halt just under the tree in which he had hidden himself. He never could have imagined that the sole person whom Jesus had come to meet was none other than he himself. Zacchaeus was amazed when Jesus called him down and informed him that He would be going to his house that day.

What followed after that was a new miracle, for which Jesus is well known: a change of heart. The cheater that Zacchaeus was now experienced a real change of heart. He had received the greatest treasure in his life in Jesus Christ, and thus all other wealth and treasures seemed futile to him. He desired to compensate all those whom he had cheated, and without waiting for the next best moment, he decided to proceed to show his faith in deeds.

Do we not rightfully sing the blessed song (written by Kent Henry) at worship, 'When I look into Your holiness, when I gaze into Your loveliness ... all things that surround become shadows." Yes! Truly before the greatness and the goodness of our Lord God all else is just a shadow. There are many rich people in the world today who are living a void life. They know and can feel the emptiness within; however, am not sure if everyone knows how to fill this void or who can make them whole. Only Christ can pull us out from our pathetic condition. Only Christ can dismount us from our throne of pride, guilt, and self-righteousness. As Jesus came and halted under the tree in which Zacchaeus was hiding, He is today speaking to you right now and desires to come to you to change you and your circumstance. You might have tasted the joy that comes from money; however, this is what the Lord says:

> And I give unto them eternal life; and they shall never perish, neither shall any man pluck them out of my hand.
>
> —John 10:28 NKJV

As salvation came into the house of Zacchaeus, so also the Lord wants to change our lives and transform us from blundermen to wondermen.

*Chapter 7*

# Prodigal Son

Born into a blessed family, the youngest son of a loving father became wayward as he followed the ways of the world. He ended up in bad company and, influenced by them, rebelled against his own father and asked for his share of the father's property. The father painfully granted it to him and was much saddened to see his son heading along the pathway of self-destruction.

Having spent all he had forced his father to give him, and after being deserted by all his friends and acquaintances, the prodigal son sought a job so he could support himself because he didn't want to die. His salary was very small—hardly enough to keep him alive. Then he remembered his generous father and recalled how even the servants in his father's house had a better living standard than his current one. Eventually, when he came to his senses, he decided to go back home. Recognizing that his pathetic condition made him undeserving, he decided to return to his father not as a son, but rather as a servant seeking employment.

It was good that he decided to return and did not finish himself off in deep sorrow and pain, for one thing is so sure and certain: God is awesomely wonderful, gracious, and compassionate, and he is a forgiver of every soul who earnestly repents for his or her sins. The prodigal son didn't even have change of clothing so he could make himself neat and tidy before approaching his father. He probably had a heavy heart and a deeply burdened mind as he headed toward his house.

Someone was waiting for him there! The father watched his son from afar and waited to embrace him and receive him back into the family. Even though no one in the family would have the same love toward this youngest son, the father could never forget and abandon his son.

It is the same way with the Heavenly Father. He loves us at all times; He will never leave us or forsake us at any time. The Father waits to bless and heal us and to forgive and restore. The moment the prodigal son's father saw his son coming, he ran to him, embraced him, and kissed him. The joy that filled the heart of the father at that time was indescribable, and then he therefore called for a celebration. Is it not rightly said in Luke 15:7 that there will be much celebration in heaven over one sinner who repents?

The son was back, reinstated in glory and honor, having received the forgiveness for his sins. He now enjoyed the bliss of his father's house.

Many people who are in similar situations to the prodigal son's situation often try to end their lives; however, there is always a chance of restoration, for our loving Father loves us so much and is always desirous to forgive and restore.

If by any chance we find ourselves in a similar situation, let this be known to us and let our hearts be well aware of this: *we have hope in God always.*

*Chapter 8*

# Saul to Paul

A devout Jew who wanted to establish by any means (even if it be by coercion) his beliefs over all was Saul, the rich, the educated, the zealot. He was a tent maker by profession, was highly educated under the great teacher Gamaliel, was a Pharisee by belief, was a Roman citizen, and was a very wealthy person. These are probably all the credentials for which we earnestly pray today—education, wealth, and prestige. Yet, Saul's soul was always in a state of unrest, and his mind was disturbed. To pacify himself and fulfill the dream of his life to preserve the sacredness of Jewish faith, he decided to obey the commands of the high priestly order to search and imprison those who were spreading Christianity, which he considered a religion based on false teaching about a god who was dead and gone; however, this god's disciples claimed that he rose again and was alive.

On his way to what Saul thought would be his next (but the Lord was about to make his last) campaign to eliminate the Christians, just as he was about to enter Damascus, he met the Light of lights, who drove away all the darkness from his life. Saul had met what he had been searching for—his perfect, loving God. Often we live in a pseudo world and accept whatever is offered, compromising and changing ourselves to fit with what we are presented with and with the way we learn we are "supposed" to feel. Yet, truly, if we yearn for more and yearn to move forward until we reach the point of ultimate satisfaction, we should carry on our yearning: Be thirsty until you quench your thirst; never abandon or abort your thirst.

Saul's quest for the true God and his encounter with the Lord Jesus were the seamless, symmetrical correlation and conglomeration. What happened after that is history: the rigid, cruel persecutor Saul turned out to be the humble, loving, persecuted disciple of Lord Jesus Christ, Paul.

It was God's perfect plan for Paul's blessedness that He planned an encounter with him and gave him an opportunity to change much more than his name, and Paul made good use of that blessed opportunity.

The Lord has a similar plan for each one of us, and we need to make use of them and glorify the Lord through our lives.

Born in Paul was a zeal to work for the kingdom of God, and he lived up to it, fulfilling it to the utmost. He did all he could do and what he was required to do; thus he boldly stated thus:

> I have fought the good fight, I have finished the race, I have kept the faith.
> —2 Timothy 4:7 NKJV

Do we ever allow the desire and quest for God in us to reach its final destination? Or do we abandon our pursuit for God in our life?

This is what the Lord God says in the Bible:

> But from there you will seek the Lord your
> God, and you will find Him if you seek
> Him with all your heart and with all your
> soul.
>
> —Deuteronomy 4:29 NKJV

Yes! The Lord is waiting for you as you search, hunger, and thirst for Him. He wants to reveal Himself to you and desires to see this happen, that the radiance of His presence will burn away the chaff in us, and we might be a renewed person living always for God's glory.

## To Know Thee More and More

Let me seek Thee, O my King
With all of my heart, my strength, my soul,
Let me ever find in Thee,
My life's ultimate and perfect goal.

Let my soul find this now,

The goodness of Your love and grace

Let my soul find rest in Thee,

As earnestly I seek Thy face.

I know I will overcome,

And more than a conqueror I'll be,

When I learn to walk in Thy perfect grace,

Thy hand of deliverance I will see

Let me not abandon this quest of mine,

A quest to know Thee more and more,

As when humbly in Thy presence I'll bow,

Like an eagle you'll make me soar.

To know Thee more and to be like Thee,

and to walk in Thy strength forever always,

Let Thy wonders amaze me ever,

Let me praise Thee all of my days.

*Chapter 9*

# Mark the Apostle

Mark the Apostle wrote the Gospel according to Mark, which wonderfully presents Jesus as the servant of all; however, Mark had to come through the hard way to be glorious for the Lord.

Mark was rejected by Paul, as told in Acts 15:38, for having deserted Paul and his people earlier in the mission field. The work of a missionary is a great blessing. Missionaries have the opportunity to tell others about the love of the Lord. They have the blessed privilege of being an instrument in God's hands to save precious souls; however, at the same time, they risk their lives for the sake of the gospel. The courage to do this comes from the Lord alone, yet some of them in some circumstances are overcome by their own wants and fears and back out from this blessed task. Human frailty and fear overcome their passion for the Lord's work.

Probably Mark also deserted the saints in this manner, and thus an outraged Paul hesitated to include him as a missionary in the next trip. So intense became the situation that Paul had to part with Barnabas because of Mark, as the ever-encouraging Barnabas could not just ignore Mark.

How often do we play different roles in similar situations—how often are we like Mark, Paul, or Barnabas?

How often are we scared and back off like Mark, later to repent with a desire to come back and partially received?

How often do we get angry like Paul and brand as "misfits" all those who cannot dare to face the adverse circumstance for the Gospel's sake?

How often are we an encourager like Barnabas who puffs life and strength into the brokenhearted, reluctant to reject and accept defeat when encountering a soul that has deserted us earlier, and also ready to give that soul a second chance until the Lord decides otherwise?

Let's be ready to return, like Mark. Let's not be angry, like Paul, and close all doors to deeds of repentance. And let's be encouragers, like Barnabas, maintaining our hope for all souls at all times.

Paul later requests that Mark join him with the following words:

> Only Luke is with me. Get Mark and bring him with you, for he is useful to me for ministry.
>
> —2 Timothy 4:11 NKJV

Having realized his earlier mistake, Paul used all the available opportunities to reconcile and bless Mark.

Thus the conclusion of the story is that a deserter changed into a helper and a useful tool for the ministry.

The one wonderful thing about the Lord our God is that He is always ready to forgive us and restore us back to our blessed calling.

If, today, anyone has thoughts similar to Mark's or finds himself or herself in a similar position to that of Mark, and if anything done in his or her past is biting the present and causing hurt, let's bring it to the Lord and get reconciled with Him, for He is ever waiting to restore us back to Himself.

Remember the example of the prodigal son who came back to his father (as mentioned in Luke chapter 15): the father was eagerly and patiently waiting for the lost son to come back.

Let us not continue in our guilt; rather, let us know that, as we have a loving and gracious Father, He is ever ready to forgive us and bless us with a fresh new beginning.

Mark, who at first was a blunderman, became a wonderman for God's glory.

*Chapter 10*

# Peter the Apostle

A fisherman by profession and a man with a hasty nature, Peter was often a failure in life. The first time he met Jesus was when he was washing his empty nets, which had been soiled after all his fishing efforts during last night had been in vain.

Peter first tasted the Lord's goodness when he received from the Lord an abundant catch in return for lending his boat to the Lord so He could deliver a blessed sermon. This itself proved to Peter—and also now speaks to us—that if we commit ourselves and all that we have to the Lord's cause, He will take care of us and bless us. He will never leave us or forsake us, for the Lord is never a debtor to anyone.

To the world, Peter might have looked like a fool who was unfit for many occasions and circumstances, yet the Lord chose him to be one of His chosen disciples. If the world rejects you and abhors you, do not consider that everything is lost or finished. The Lord has His eye upon you, and He will lift you up at the right time, for this is what the precious Lord tells us:

> But God has chosen the foolish things of the world to put to shame the wise, and God has chosen the weak things of the world to put to shame the things which are mighty.
>
> 1 Corinthians 1:27 NKJV

For the entire three and a half years Peter was with the Lord, witnessing every great and small thing the Lord did, he was also close to the Lord and thus loved the Lord abundantly. He had left his work and profession at the Lord's call and spent time with the Lord, learning from Him and being blessed, and thus, due to the nature that he possessed, he betrayed the Lord three times to save himself, wept bitterly having done so, went back to his profession as a fisherman again to experience the same miracle, and later became the pioneer of the early church, filled with the Holy Spirit, working wonders and miracles for God's glory.

The life of the Apostle Peter is a wonderful example of the Lord's love and concern for all. The Lord God selected and elected Peter for His glory.

The Lord transformed Peter from a coward who betrayed the Lord into a bold preacher who was ultimately martyred for the Lord.

The Lord transformed an ordinary fisherman into an efficient fisher of men as promised.

The Lord transformed him from an ordinary man to a man filled with the Holy Spirit working wonders for the Lord.

*Chapter 11*

# Saint Augustine

Born into a rich family with a devout, believing mother, Saint Monica, and a pagan father, Patricius, who converted to Christianity on his deathbed, Augustine literally wasted his life in sin. He almost destroyed and wasted his life in all the worldly indulgences and vile habits.

What could happen to such a soul, which was lost in all of the worldly affairs? Was there a force that could pull him out of this dungeon of death?

God's mercy and grace were directed toward Augustine as a result of his mother's prayers, and when he was convicted by the Holy Spirit of the sinful life he was living, Augustine committed himself to the Lord to be used for His glory, who worked in him for good. That is how the world now knows this man as Saint Augustine.

If you know of anyone who has gone away from the Lord or is living a deranged life, you should know that there is hope in the Lord for him or her. If we are ready to pray like Augustine's mother, we may have the Lord's mercy extended to those souls who do not know the Lord God.

Augustine's life is similar to that of the life of the prodigal son, and this story keeps repeating even today when the benevolent prayers of the saints have saved their loved ones, and lives have been transformed for God's glory.

# Chapter 12

# John Newton, Writer of the Hymn "Amazing Grace"

John Newton was an English sailor and a slave trader who later received the Lord as His personal Savior. He wrote one of the most famous hymns in the English language, "Amazing Grace."

Having experienced a difficult and bitter childhood, Newton grew up to be a brutal slave trader bringing in slaves from Africa to the Western countries. His trade was sinful and against the will of God.

Later, on one occasion when he was working as the captain of a slave ship, his ship was overtaken by an enormous storm, he miraculously experienced the mighty hand of Lord God; the Lord changed his life and made him a humble person. The transformation resulted in his salvation, and soon the fruits of the Spirit were seen in his life. He who had promoted slavery and was himself a slave trader now worked for the abolition of slavery and saw the results of his efforts within his lifetime.

Newton also wrote the blessed song, "Amazing Grace," which has been and will continue to be a blessing for many souls.

His story is similar to that of Saint Paul, who earlier had been a persecutor of the church and Christianity, but who later gave himself up and worked for the church and to spread Christianity.

This wonderful experience teaches us that nothing is impossible with God, for He can transform every soul and save him or her for eternal glory.

We see in our day-to-day lives so many people indulging in and involving themselves in all the vile activities and sinful ways of the world. They love to do what they do—violence, theft, immoral ways, and so forth. Yet, if they could experience the salvation of the Lord as Newton did, they too would become abhorrers of sin and evil and lovers of all that is good and sacred.

The Lord's desire for all is that we should be saved, and when His wonderful plan unfolds in each life, we see the wonderful and blessed fruits of the Spirit— the previous person being renewed and the new and blessed person emerging with a transformed life.

There are many people who are similar to John Newton, who actually are a nuisance to many, yet if the Lord God could change them, transform them, they would be a blessing to all.

The blunderman John Newton, the persecutor of the slaves, became a wonderman, composing blessed songs for the Lord and ministering to many precious souls.

*Chapter 13*

# Conclusion

The Lord created wondermen in His image; however, the devil transformed them to blundermen. Yet the Lord desires to restore each of us to the blessed position of a blessed person.

With the examples I have shared, we have seen that the Lord can transform and restore. I would like to reiterate what I said in the beginning of this book from the blessed hymn written by Stuart Hamblen, which says:

> It is no secret what God can do,
>
> What He's done for others, He will do for you.
>
> With arms wide open, He will pardon you.
>
> It is no secret what God can do.

Commit your life and circumstance into the Lord's hands, and let Him change you in His own blessed way to be the wonderman or wonderwoman He has always desired you to be.